M000196680

# MINDFULNESS JOURNAL

# MIND
# FULN
# JOU

Writing Rituals for Self-Discovery,
Clarity, and Joy

ROHAN GUNATILLAKE

CHRONICLE BOOKS
SAN FRANCISCO

ISBN 978-1-7972-1975-2

Manufactured in China.

Design by Tonje Vetleseter.
Typeset in Whitney.

10 9 8 7 6 5 4 3 2 1

Chronicle Books publishes distinctive books and gifts. From award-winning children's titles, bestselling cookbooks, and eclectic pop culture to acclaimed works of art and design, stationery, and journals, we craft publishing that's instantly recognizable for its spirit and creativity. Enjoy our publishing and become part of our community at www.chroniclebooks.com.

Special quantity discounts are available to corporations and other organizations. Contact our premiums department at corporatesales@chroniclebooks.com or at 1-800-759-0190.

Chronicle Books LLC
680 Second Street
San Francisco, California 94107
www.chroniclebooks.com

## WELCOME TO YOUR MINDFULNESS JOURNAL

---

I have been practicing and teaching mindfulness for close to two decades, and writing and reflection have been central to developing my practice. Taking something internal to ourselves—a thought, a feeling, a sensation—and then expressing it as an observed experience is the heart of mindfulness.

This journal is designed to encourage a regular mindfulness practice so that you can experience calm, clarity, and joy. On each spread, you'll find a journaling prompt, a writing invitation based on practices I've explored in many years of studying and sharing mindfulness with people around the world. Whether you are new to journaling or an old hand, or whether you are new to mindfulness or a seasoned meditator, you will find some treasure here. And most importantly, that treasure will come from you, from your hand, your mind, and the natural wisdom that comes with reflection.

The prompts are organized around five qualities at the heart of mindfulness practice:

KINDNESS: To encourage connection and gratitude.

AWARENESS: To tune into the present moment and see the beauty in the world around you.

STILLNESS: To support rest and calm.

WISDOM: To encourage deep thinking and contemplation.

CURIOSITY: To cultivate a sense of wonder and possibility.

Each prompt appears twice, giving you a chance to notice the ways your experience of the prompt and your response change depending on the day, your mood, and the quality of your mind. You can use the prompts in different ways: Begin or end your day with one, answer one a week, or pick one whenever you feel like it. You can take them in order or pick one at random. Make it your own.

Most importantly, have fun with this experience and be gentle on yourself. As thoughts and feelings arise, notice and record them without judgment or labels. Take things at your own pace, and follow your instinct and what brings you a sense of joy and play. I've always found that my own practice has been at its best when there is real lightness.

Enjoy the journey ahead. Reflecting on what we observe so that we truly learn from what we see is the heart of wisdom. I'm excited for what may emerge from your time spent here and wish you all the best in your adventures in mindfulness, with this journal and beyond.

—Rohan Gunatillake

With your face and jaw comfortable and relaxed, close your eyes and spend a few moments just listening. Count how many sounds you can hear. What is near? What is far? Notice the quality of each noise. Open your eyes and journal about what you heard in as much detail as possible. What does it feel like to bring all your attention to listening?

_____

_____

_____

_____

_____

_____

_____

_____

_____

_____

_____

_____

_____

_____

Bringing our attention to the kindness of strangers encourages us to zoom out a bit and see ourselves as part of a greater whole. What is the kindest thing that a stranger has ever done for you? Write about it—how it made you feel at the time and how you feel about it now.

_____

_____

_____

_____

_____

_____

_____

_____

_____

_____

_____

_____

_____

_____

_____

_____

_____

Sitting with a straight back and a soft belly helps us embody the qualities of mindfulness. A straight back encourages alertness and brightness, and a soft belly fosters a sense of relaxation and openness. Practice sitting in this position now, gently repeating "Straight back, soft belly" in your mind. Sit quietly for a few moments in this position, then journal about what comes up.

_____

_____

_____

_____

_____

_____

_____

_____

_____

_____

_____

_____

_____

Bring your attention to the loveliest thing that happened to you in the last week, however small, and journal about it below. It could be a kindness, a moment of connection, or a personal win. Our minds tend to prioritize the not-so-good aspects of experience, but we don't need to give those things any more energy. Practice focusing on the lovely things that bring joy.

_____

_____

_____

_____

_____

_____

_____

_____

_____

_____

_____

_____

_____

_____

Our breath and our state of mind are interconnected, and the quality of one can impact the other. Spend a few moments sitting quietly. Bring your attention to your breath and describe the quality of it below. Next, spend a few moments observing your thoughts. Notice your mind and where your thoughts wander, and describe those too. Then explore how your breath and mind are connected and how they influence one another.

_____

_____

_____

_____

_____

_____

_____

_____

_____

_____

_____

_____

_____

Bringing our attention to the wide web of people that impact our day-to-day experiences helps us see ourselves as part of a greater, interconnected world. Think of your favorite drink—coffee, tea, wine, water, or whatever it might be. List as many people as you can who have played their part in getting it to you, while imagining as many details as possible. Extend gratitude to each person as you add them to this page.

_____

_____

_____

_____

_____

_____

_____

_____

_____

_____

_____

_____

_____

_____

Bring your awareness to the quality of your mind in this moment, then describe it below. For example, is your mind roving or still? Playing a tune? Fixated on a single thought? Don't overthink; write whatever comes up. Emotions, colors, sounds—jot it all down.

_____

_____

_____

_____

_____

_____

_____

_____

_____

_____

_____

_____

_____

_____

However noisy the space is around you or however noisy your own mind is, you can always access calm. Find a point of stillness—a book on a shelf, a mug on your desk, a tree outside your window—and let your attention rest there for several moments. What does it feel like to tune into stillness?

_____

_____

_____

_____

_____

_____

_____

_____

_____

_____

_____

_____

_____

_____

_____

_____

Letting go is an idea central to mindfulness. When we let go of things like expectation, control, or attachment, we release ourselves from the pain and suffering that come with them. What might you let go of today? Maybe it's frustration, a plan, or even a relationship. What emotions come up when you imagine letting go?

_____

_____

_____

_____

_____

_____

_____

_____

_____

_____

_____

_____

_____

_____

Often, we are better at being kind to others than being kind to ourselves. In this exercise, you'll practice sending yourself loving-kindness; this is a mindful practice designed to cultivate compassion. Below, write down the phrase "May I be well, may I be happy" three times, and then journal about how that phrase makes you feel. What comes to mind when you imagine feeling well and happy? How does it feel to show yourself kindness?

_____

_____

_____

_____

_____

_____

_____

_____

_____

_____

_____

_____

_____

_____

Our senses allow us to explore the world through hearing, feeling, smelling, seeing, and tasting. Spend a few moments tuning in to each individual sense, and notice what happens when you give all your attention to that one facet of your experience. What is it like to focus deeply on one sense at a time?

_____

_____

_____

_____

_____

_____

_____

_____

_____

_____

_____

_____

_____

_____

One way to avoid getting stuck in the stories that run through your mind is to learn to watch your mind like you're watching TV. This practice creates a bit of distance between you and the narrative. To do this practice, close your eyes and consider what "show" is on at the moment—what story has been demanding your attention recently? Who are the main characters, and what is the storyline? Journal about the "show" and what it feels like to take a step back and observe this narrative from afar.

_____

_____

_____

_____

_____

_____

_____

_____

_____

_____

_____

_____

With so many things demanding our attention all day, it's rare for our minds to have nothing to do. Find a quiet place to sit and spend at least ten minutes putting all distractions aside—silence your phone, turn off any music or TV, and close your email inbox. See what happens when you gift yourself silence and stillness. Without judgment, notice what comes up, and then journal about the experience below.

The connections and pathways in our brains change over the course of our lives based on how we think, what we do, and where we are. Our brains are constantly making new connections and pathways, which means that we are always training ourselves in something—whether we're aware of it or not. What qualities in yourself do you want to develop, and how can you begin practicing those things today?

_____

_____

_____

_____

_____

_____

_____

_____

_____

_____

_____

_____

_____

_____

We can hold a lot of wisdom in our physicality, but we don't always take the time to listen. Spend a few moments with your eyes closed, tuning in to your body. Slowly scan your body, from the tips of your toes to the top of your head. Notice where there is tension, pain, or relaxation. What is your body telling you? Write about what you discover.

Asking "How can I love more?" invites us to connect more deeply in all our relationships. Sometimes this will mean putting more energy into being present or generous even when you don't feel like it. Spend a few minutes writing about how you can love more—whether that's by being more present, showing generosity, expressing words of affirmation, or taking another action. However love manifests, loving more is a beautiful way to engage with your world.

_____

_____

_____

_____

_____

_____

_____

_____

_____

_____

_____

_____

_____

Nature is all around us, in small and big ways. Bringing our attention to nature is a beautiful way to practice mindfulness and connect with the present moment. Spend a few moments bringing your awareness to the nature around you—clouds passing overhead, tree leaves rustling nearby, the sound of birds or wind outside. How does it feel to bring your attention to nature? How might you incorporate small moments of nature into your life in the days ahead?

_____

_____

_____

_____

_____

_____

_____

_____

_____

_____

_____

_____

_____

Boredom is often seen as something to avoid, but it can be an opportunity for calm and stillness. Below, journal about what boredom feels like to you—in your mind and your body. Notice what qualities you associate with boredom, and consider how moments of boredom might be transformed into opportunities to embrace stillness.

_____

_____

_____

_____

_____

_____

_____

_____

_____

_____

_____

_____

_____

_____

_____

Much of the difficulty we encounter in our day-to-day lives results from our desire to always be in control. We are upset when a plan falls apart, a person doesn't live up to our expectations, or a conversation doesn't go as we'd expected. What would it be like to relax our need to be in charge of what happens to us and other people? Journal about how you feel when you imagine releasing control.

_____

_____

_____

_____

_____

_____

_____

_____

_____

_____

_____

_____

_____

When we practice mindful awareness, we begin to see the connections between our circumstances and the quality of our mind. *When that happens, this also happens; when life is like this, I am like that.* How is your mood right now? And how is it connected to other parts of your day, your life, or the space around you?

_____

_____

_____

_____

_____

_____

_____

_____

_____

_____

_____

_____

_____

_____

_____

While it can be the easier option to say no to things to pro-tect our energy and our time, sometimes we say no because we're operating from a place of fear or closemindedness. Where in your life can you say yes more? Close your eyes and imagine your mind being a "yes" mind—whatever that might mean to you. What does that feel like?

We can sometimes believe we are not worthy of kindness. A powerful first step to free yourself from your feelings of unworthiness is to begin naming the things that make you feel unworthy. Calling them by their names whenever they appear helps you create a little bit of distance between you and them and avoid getting entangled in an unproductive thought spiral. Below, write out the things that make you feel unworthy or undeserving. Without judgment, see what comes up.

Our connection to the ground is always available to us. By simply paying attention to the feeling of our feet, we can literally ground ourselves at any time and bring our awareness back to the present moment. Spend five minutes sitting with your feet planted on the floor. Notice the connection between your body and the ground below you. Write about how your body and mind felt in that experience.

_____

_____

_____

_____

_____

_____

_____

_____

_____

_____

_____

_____

_____

_____

Distractions can pull us out of the present moment and make it difficult to practice stillness. Consider what distractions have been demanding your attention recently, and list them below. Then journal about what you can do to stay in the moment when distraction pulls at your attention.

_____

_____

_____

_____

_____

_____

_____

_____

_____

_____

_____

_____

_____

_____

_____

Living well in a digital world can be difficult. Describe your own relationship with technology and, more importantly, how you might bring a greater level of awareness to how you engage with your devices. Are there small steps you can take today to live a more mindful digital life?

_____

_____

_____

_____

_____

_____

_____

_____

_____

_____

_____

_____

_____

_____

_____

_____

Asking the question "Where is my mind now?" is an effective way to bring yourself back into present awareness. Close your eyes and spend a minute observing where your mind is in the present moment, then write about what comes up. Repeat this three times in a row. Look back through your notes, seeing where your mind wandered when left to its own devices. Was it all over the place? Focused on the same thing? Be curious about what you observe.

Celebrating the joy of others can help us cultivate joy in ourselves. Yet when a lovely thing happens to another person, often our first reaction is to feel jealous or wonder why things like that don't happen to us. Practicing sympathetic joy is a way to help rewire our brains so that we default to joy instead of more negative thoughts. For this exercise, think of someone you know who has had recent success, and then spend five minutes writing about how their happiness brings you happiness.

_____

_____

_____

_____

_____

_____

_____

_____

_____

_____

_____

_____

_____

Writing with a pen or pencil is a lovely way of connecting your mind to an object through your body and then using that object to express your mind. Bring your awareness to the act of writing. Using the space below, write about what the act of writing feels like in as much detail as possible. Describe the sensations in your fingers, the movement in your hands, and the feeling of contact with the paper.

Mindfulness asks us to "just be." Though it may seem simple, this act of just being can be a challenge. Spend five minutes today practicing just being, doing your best to keep your attention on the present moment without distraction. Then journal about how this feels.

_____

_____

_____

_____

_____

_____

_____

_____

_____

_____

_____

_____

_____

_____

_____

Spend some time freewriting in the space below. Don't hold back or overthink; just see what happens when you put pen to paper and follow one thought to the next. When you've finished writing, read through what you've written and notice where your mind naturally gravitates.

_____

_____

_____

_____

_____

_____

_____

_____

_____

_____

_____

_____

_____

_____

_____

_____

Though we are often quick to say thank you to others when they offer us kindness or support, we rarely say thank you to ourselves. We are so deserving of our own gratitude. Think of the things you do, big and small, to care for yourself and get through each day. Make a list of as many things as possible, and then read it back to yourself and say thank you as you read each item.

_____

_____

_____

_____

_____

_____

_____

_____

_____

_____

_____

_____

_____

_____

There is so much beauty in the delicate—feathers, snow-flakes, spider webs. Today, pick something delicate and spend five minutes meditating on that, imagining it in as much detail as possible. Then consider how you can move through life with that same delicacy, engaging fully with the reality of the world around you but with an approach that is more like a feather than a brick. What does it feel like to imagine approaching the world with such lightness?

_____

_____

_____

_____

_____

_____

_____

_____

_____

_____

_____

_____

_____

We are constantly making decisions. Some are minor everyday choices, like what shirt to wear or what to cook for dinner, and others are more significant and life changing, like what job to take or where to put down roots. When it comes to making decisions, our bodies are full of wisdom, so taking the time to check in with how our bodies feel can give us access to information that we often overlook. Think of a decision, big or small, and give yourself a few minutes to sit quietly. Write about what you notice when you check in with your body, and how that might inform the choice at hand.

_____

_____

_____

_____

_____

_____

_____

_____

_____

_____

_____

_____

As we practice mindful awareness, the question of awareness becomes increasingly prominent. When we can start to observe our thoughts from a distance, we become more curious about who we are if not our thoughts. Spend a few minutes sitting with this question and journaling about what comes up in your mind.

_____

_____

_____

_____

_____

_____

_____

_____

_____

_____

_____

_____

_____

_____

With your face and jaw comfortable and relaxed, close your eyes and spend a few moments just listening. Count how many sounds you can hear. What is near? What is far? Notice the quality of each noise. Open your eyes and journal about what you heard in as much detail as possible. What does it feel like to bring all your attention to listening?

---

---

---

---

---

---

---

---

---

---

---

---

Bringing our attention to the kindness of strangers encourages us to zoom out a bit and see ourselves as part of a greater whole. What is the kindest thing that a stranger has ever done for you? Write about it—how it made you feel at the time and how you feel about it now.

_____

_____

_____

_____

_____

_____

_____

_____

_____

_____

_____

_____

_____

_____

_____

_____

Sitting with a straight back and a soft belly helps us embody the qualities of mindfulness. A straight back encourages alertness and brightness, and a soft belly fosters a sense of relaxation and openness. Practice sitting in this position now, gently repeating "Straight back, soft belly" in your mind. Sit quietly for a few moments in this position, then journal about what comes up.

_____

_____

_____

_____

_____

_____

_____

_____

_____

_____

_____

_____

_____

Bring your attention to the loveliest thing that happened to you in the last week, however small, and journal about it below. It could be a kindness, a moment of connection, or a personal win. Our minds tend to prioritize the not-so-good aspects of experience, but we don't need to give those things any more energy. Practice focusing on the lovely things that bring joy.

_____

_____

_____

_____

_____

_____

_____

_____

_____

_____

_____

_____

_____

_____

Our breath and our state of mind are interconnected, and the quality of one can impact the other. Spend a few moments sitting quietly. Bring your attention to your breath and describe the quality of it below. Next, spend a few moments observing your thoughts. Notice your mind and where your thoughts wander, and describe those too. Then explore how your breath and mind are connected and how they influence one another.

_____

_____

_____

_____

_____

_____

_____

_____

_____

_____

_____

_____

_____

_____

_____

Bringing our attention to the wide web of people that impact our day-to-day experiences helps us see ourselves as part of a greater, interconnected world. Think of your favorite drink—coffee, tea, wine, water, or whatever it might be. List as many people as you can who have played their part in getting it to you, while imagining as many details as possible. Extend gratitude to each person as you add them to this page.

_____

_____

_____

_____

_____

_____

_____

_____

_____

_____

_____

_____

_____

_____

_____

Bring your awareness to the quality of your mind in this moment, then describe it below. For example, is your mind roving or still? Playing a tune? Fixated on a single thought? Don't overthink; write whatever comes up. Emotions, colors, sounds—jot it all down.

_____

_____

_____

_____

_____

_____

_____

_____

_____

_____

_____

_____

_____

_____

_____

_____

However noisy the space is around you or however noisy your own mind is, you can always access calm. Find a point of stillness—a book on a shelf, a mug on your desk, a tree outside your window—and let your attention rest there for several moments. What does it feel like to tune into stillness?

_____

_____

_____

_____

_____

_____

_____

_____

_____

_____

_____

_____

_____

_____

Letting go is an idea central to mindfulness. When we let go of things like expectation, control, or attachment, we release ourselves from the pain and suffering that come with them. What might you let go of today? Maybe it's frustration, a plan, or even a relationship. What emotions come up when you imagine letting go?

_____

_____

_____

_____

_____

_____

_____

_____

_____

_____

_____

_____

_____

_____

Often, we are better at being kind to others than being kind to ourselves. In this exercise, you'll practice sending yourself loving-kindness; this is a mindful practice designed to cultivate compassion. Below, write down the phrase "May I be well, may I be happy" three times, and then journal about how that phrase makes you feel. What comes to mind when you imagine feeling well and happy? How does it feel to show yourself kindness?

_____

_____

_____

_____

_____

_____

_____

_____

_____

_____

_____

_____

_____

_____

Our senses allow us to explore the world through hearing, feeling, smelling, seeing, and tasting. Spend a few moments tuning in to each individual sense, and notice what happens when you give all your attention to that one facet of your experience. What is it like to focus deeply on one sense at a time?

_____

_____

_____

_____

_____

_____

_____

_____

_____

_____

_____

_____

_____

_____

_____

_____

One way to avoid getting stuck in the stories that run through your mind is to learn to watch your mind like you're watching TV. This practice creates a bit of distance between you and the narrative. To do this practice, close your eyes and consider what "show" is on at the moment— what story has been demanding your attention recently? Who are the main characters, and what is the storyline? Journal about the "show" and what it feels like to take a step back and observe this narrative from afar.

With so many things demanding our attention all day, it's rare for our minds to have nothing to do. Find a quiet place to sit and spend at least ten minutes putting all distractions aside—silence your phone, turn off any music or TV, and close your email inbox. See what happens when you gift yourself silence and stillness. Without judgment, notice what comes up, and then journal about the experience below.

The connections and pathways in our brains change over the course of our lives based on how we think, what we do, and where we are. Our brains are constantly making new connections and pathways, which means that we are always training ourselves in something—whether we're aware of it or not. What qualities in yourself do you want to develop, and how can you begin practicing those things today?

_____

_____

_____

_____

_____

_____

_____

_____

_____

_____

_____

_____

_____

_____

We can hold a lot of wisdom in our physicality, but we don't always take the time to listen. Spend a few moments with your eyes closed, tuning in to your body. Slowly scan your body, from the tips of your toes to the top of your head. Notice where there is tension, pain, or relaxation. What is your body telling you? Write about what you discover.

Asking "How can I love more?" invites us to connect more deeply in all our relationships. Sometimes this will mean putting more energy into being present or generous even when you don't feel like it. Spend a few minutes writing about how you can love more—whether that's by being more present, showing generosity, expressing words of affirmation, or taking another action. However love manifests, loving more is a beautiful way to engage with your world.

_____

_____

_____

_____

_____

_____

_____

_____

_____

_____

_____

_____

_____

_____

Nature is all around us, in small and big ways. Bringing our attention to nature is a beautiful way to practice mindfulness and connect with the present moment. Spend a few moments bringing your awareness to the nature around you—clouds passing overhead, tree leaves rustling nearby, the sound of birds or wind outside. How does it feel to bring your attention to nature? How might you incorporate small moments of nature into your life in the days ahead?

_____

_____

_____

_____

_____

_____

_____

_____

_____

_____

_____

_____

_____

Boredom is often seen as something to avoid, but it can be an opportunity for calm and stillness. Below, journal about what boredom feels like to you—in your mind and your body. Notice what qualities you associate with boredom, and consider how moments of boredom might be transformed into opportunities to embrace stillness.

_____

_____

_____

_____

_____

_____

_____

_____

_____

_____

_____

_____

_____

_____

Much of the difficulty we encounter in our day-to-day lives results from our desire to always be in control. We are upset when a plan falls apart, a person doesn't live up to our expectations, or a conversation doesn't go as we'd expected. What would it be like to relax our need to be in charge of what happens to us and other people? Journal about how you feel when you imagine releasing control.

_____

_____

_____

_____

_____

_____

_____

_____

_____

_____

_____

_____

_____

_____

When we practice mindful awareness, we begin to see the connections between our circumstances and the quality of our mind. *When that happens, this also happens; when life is like this, I am like that.* How is your mood right now? And how is it connected to other parts of your day, your life, or the space around you?

_____

_____

_____

_____

_____

_____

_____

_____

_____

_____

_____

_____

_____

_____

_____

While it can be the easier option to say no to things to protect our energy and our time, sometimes we say no because we're operating from a place of fear or closemindedness. Where in your life can you say yes more? Close your eyes and imagine your mind being a "yes" mind—whatever that might mean to you. What does that feel like?

_____

_____

_____

_____

_____

_____

_____

_____

_____

_____

_____

_____

_____

_____

We can sometimes believe we are not worthy of kindness. A powerful first step to free yourself from your feelings of unworthiness is to begin naming the things that make you feel unworthy. Calling them by their names whenever they appear helps you create a little bit of distance between you and them and avoid getting entangled in an unproductive thought spiral. Below, write out the things that make you feel unworthy or undeserving. Without judgment, see what comes up.

_____

_____

_____

_____

_____

_____

_____

_____

_____

_____

_____

_____

_____

_____

Our connection to the ground is always available to us. By simply paying attention to the feeling of our feet, we can literally ground ourselves at any time and bring our awareness back to the present moment. Spend five minutes sitting with your feet planted on the floor. Notice the connection between your body and the ground below you. Write about how your body and mind felt in that experience.

_____

_____

_____

_____

_____

_____

_____

_____

_____

_____

_____

_____

_____

_____

Distractions can pull us out of the present moment and make it difficult to practice stillness. Consider what distractions have been demanding your attention recently, and list them below. Then journal about what you can do to stay in the moment when distraction pulls at your attention.

_____

_____

_____

_____

_____

_____

_____

_____

_____

_____

_____

_____

_____

_____

_____

Living well in a digital world can be difficult. Describe your own relationship with technology and, more importantly, how you might bring a greater level of awareness to how you engage with your devices. Are there small steps you can take today to live a more mindful digital life?

_____

_____

_____

_____

_____

_____

_____

_____

_____

_____

_____

_____

_____

_____

_____

_____

_____

Asking the question "Where is my mind now?" is an effective way to bring yourself back into present awareness. Close your eyes and spend a minute observing where your mind is in the present moment, then write about what comes up. Repeat this three times in a row. Look back through your notes, seeing where your mind wandered when left to its own devices. Was it all over the place? Focused on the same thing? Be curious about what you observe.

_____

_____

_____

_____

_____

_____

_____

_____

_____

_____

_____

_____

_____

_____

Celebrating the joy of others can help us cultivate joy in ourselves. Yet when a lovely thing happens to another person, often our first reaction is to feel jealous or wonder why things like that don't happen to us. Practicing sympathetic joy is a way to help rewire our brains so that we default to joy instead of more negative thoughts. For this exercise, think of someone you know who has had recent success, and then spend five minutes writing about how their happiness brings you happiness.

Writing with a pen or pencil is a lovely way of connecting your mind to an object through your body and then using that object to express your mind. Bring your awareness to the act of writing. Using the space below, write about what the act of writing feels like in as much detail as possible. Describe the sensations in your fingers, the movement in your hands, and the feeling of contact with the paper.

_____

_____

_____

_____

_____

_____

_____

_____

_____

_____

_____

_____

_____

Mindfulness asks us to "just be." Though it may seem simple, this act of just being can be a challenge. Spend five minutes today practicing just being, doing your best to keep your attention on the present moment without distraction. Then journal about how this feels.

_____

_____

_____

_____

_____

_____

_____

_____

_____

_____

_____

_____

_____

_____

Spend some time freewriting in the space below. Don't hold back or overthink; just see what happens when you put pen to paper and follow one thought to the next. When you've finished writing, read through what you've written and notice where your mind naturally gravitates.

_____

_____

_____

_____

_____

_____

_____

_____

_____

_____

_____

_____

_____

_____

_____

_____

Though we are often quick to say thank you to others when they offer us kindness or support, we rarely say thank you to ourselves. We are so deserving of our own gratitude. Think of the things you do, big and small, to care for yourself and get through each day. Make a list of as many things as possible, and then read it back to yourself and say thank you as you read each item.

There is so much beauty in the delicate—feathers, snow-flakes, spider webs. Today, pick something delicate and spend five minutes meditating on that, imagining it in as much detail as possible. Then consider how you can move through life with that same delicacy, engaging fully with the reality of the world around you but with an approach that is more like a feather than a brick. What does it feel like to imagine approaching the world with such lightness?

We are constantly making decisions. Some are minor everyday choices, like what shirt to wear or what to cook for dinner, and others are more significant and life changing, like what job to take or where to put down roots. When it comes to making decisions, our bodies are full of wisdom, so taking the time to check in with how our bodies feel can give us access to information that we often overlook. Think of a decision, big or small, and give yourself a few minutes to sit quietly. Write about what you notice when you check in with your body, and how that might inform the choice at hand.

_____

_____

_____

_____

_____

_____

_____

_____

_____

_____

_____

As we practice mindful awareness, the question of awareness becomes increasingly prominent. When we can start
to observe our thoughts from a distance, we become more
curious about who we are if not our thoughts. Spend a few
minutes sitting with this question and journaling about what
comes up in your mind.

_____

_____

_____

_____

_____

_____

_____

_____

_____

_____

_____

_____

_____

_____

_____